HOW TO PAINT BY STICKER

1. PICK YOUR IMAGE.
Find the sticker map of the image you want to paint with stickers. Do you want to sticker a rover exploring the surface of Mars or an astronaut on a spacewalk? It's up to you!

STICKER MAP

2. FIND YOUR STICKERS.
The sticker sheets are in the back of the book. Use the image in the top corner of each sheet to help you find the one that matches the picture you want to paint. Both the sticker sheets and the sticker maps can be torn out of the book so you don't have to flip back and forth between them.

STICKER SHEET

3. MATCH THE NUMBERS.
Each sticker has a number underneath it, and each sticker map has numbers on it. Match the sticker number with the number on the painting page. Be careful! The stickers aren't removable.

56

4. WATCH YOUR PAINTING COME TO LIFE!
After you've finished your masterpiece, you can frame it, use it as decoration, or give it as a gift.

ARE YOU READY? LET'S START STICKERING!

PAINT BY STICKER

KIDS

OUTER SPACE

workman

• NEW YORK •

Copyright © 2021 by Workman Publishing Co., Inc.

All rights reserved. No portion of this book may be reproduced—mechanically, electronically, or by any other means, including photocopying—without written permission of the publisher. Published simultaneously in Canada by Thomas Allen & Son Limited.

Library of Congress Cataloging-in-Publication Data is available.

ISBN 978-1-5235-1301-7

Design by Ying Cheng

The 10 low-poly images in this book are based on illustrations by Ying Cheng.

Workman books are available at special discounts when purchased in bulk for premiums and sales promotions as well as for fundraising or educational use. Special editions or book excerpts can also be created to specification. For details, contact the Special Sales Director at specialmarkets@workman.com.

Workman Publishing Co., Inc.
225 Varick Street
New York, NY 10014-4381

workman.com

WORKMAN and PAINT BY STICKER are registered trademarks of Workman Publishing Co., Inc.

Printed in China on paper from responsible sources
First printing April 2021

10 9 8 7 6 5 4 3

ROCKET SHIP

A rocket ship is a vehicle powered by rockets that takes people to space. In 1961, Yuri Gagarin became the first human to go to space in a rocket ship called *Vostok 1*. The rocket ship pictured is called a space shuttle. NASA used space shuttles to take astronauts to space until 2011.

MOON

Many scientists believe that billions of years ago, an object the size of Mars smashed into Earth, creating bits and pieces that eventually formed Earth's moon. In 1962, NASA mathematician Katherine Johnson used geometry to figure out how to travel to the moon. Seven years later, Neil Armstrong became the first astronaut to set foot on the moon's surface.

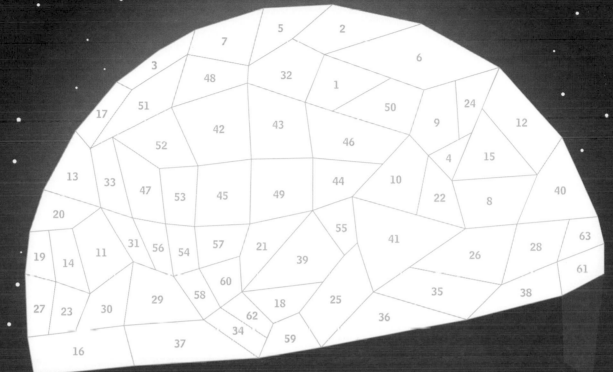

EARTH

Earth is an ocean planet—water covers more than 70 percent of the Earth's surface. It is also the only known planet in the universe where living things, like plants and animals, exist.

JUPITER

Jupiter is known for the Great Red Spot, a giant storm that's more than 150 years old. The storm is twice as wide as the Earth, and it changes size and shape as it swirls.

ASTRONAUT

An astronaut is a person who is trained to travel into space. In space, astronauts wear specially designed space suits that keep them cool and give them air to breathe. Some space suits even have jet packs that let astronauts fly!

SATURN

Saturn is surrounded by thousands of rings made of rock, water, and ice. When the sun shines through the rings, they sparkle!

SUN

All of the planets in our solar system orbit around the Sun. The Sun is a star made of hot gas that gives the Earth heat and light. Sunlight is made of many colors. You can see some of them when the Sun shines through the rain and makes a rainbow.

MARS ROVER

A rover is a spacecraft that is designed to explore the surfaces of other planets and collect data. A Mars rover named *Curiosity* found remnants of an ancient streambed and rocks that were exposed to water billions of years ago, proving that there was once water on Mars!

OBSERVATORY

An observatory is a building that has powerful telescopes and other tools used to observe space. The roof opens so the telescopes can point up at the sky! This observatory is studying the constellations Ursa Major (the Big Dipper) and Ursa Minor (the Little Dipper).

COMET

Comets are balls of ice, rock, gas, and dust that zoom around the Sun. When their orbit brings them close to the Sun, they heat up and start to spew a trail of dust and gas. Sometimes this trail can stretch for millions of miles!

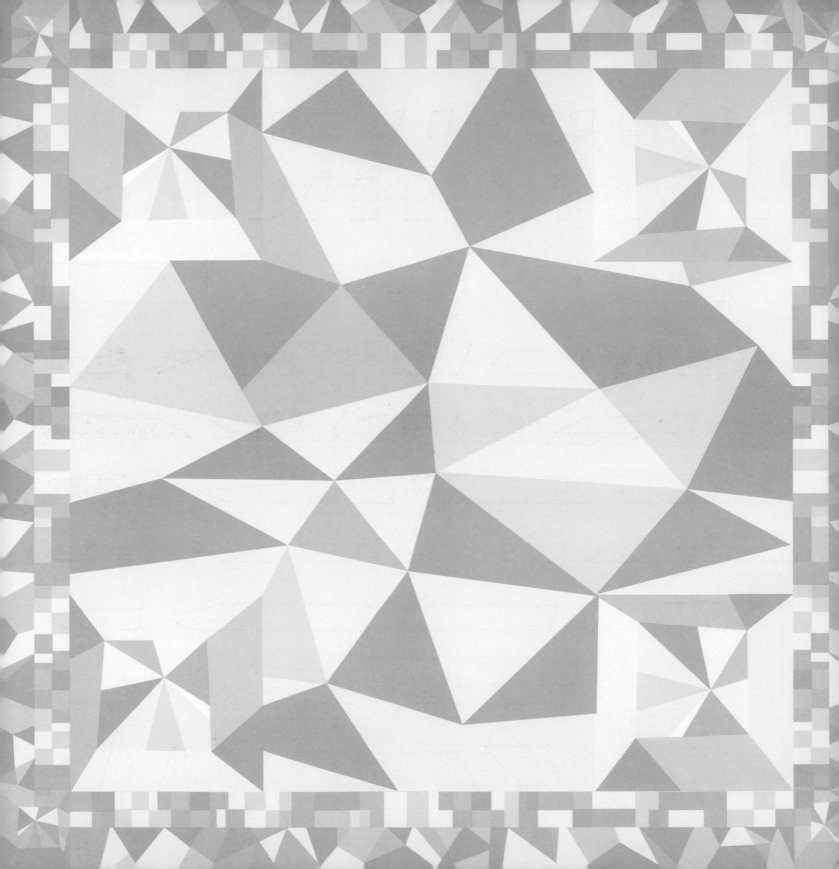

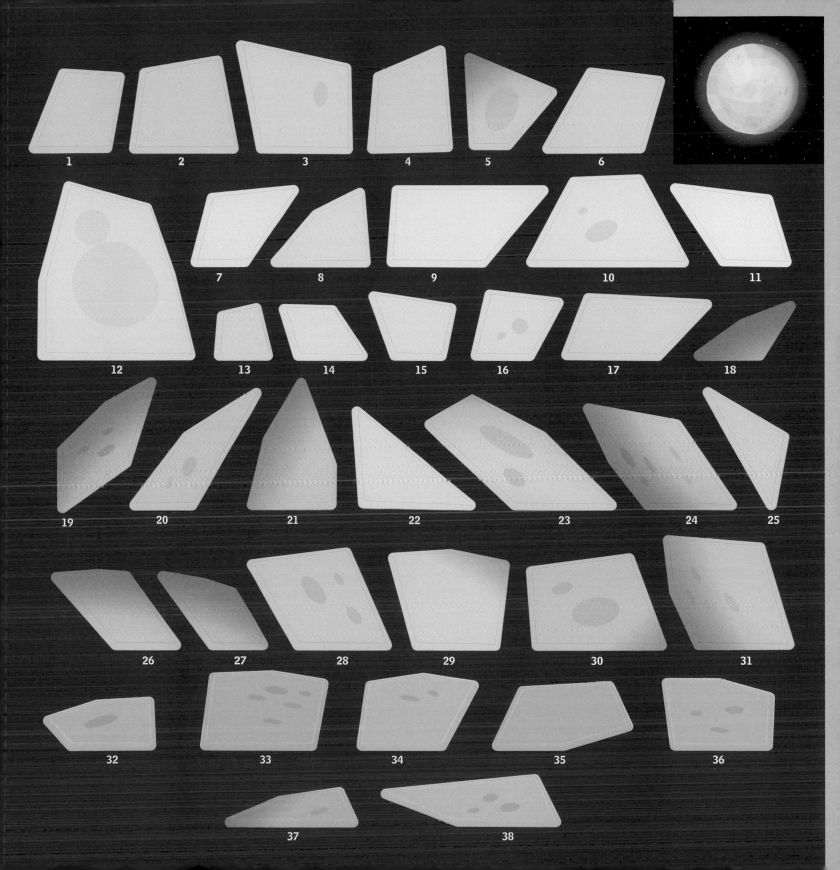

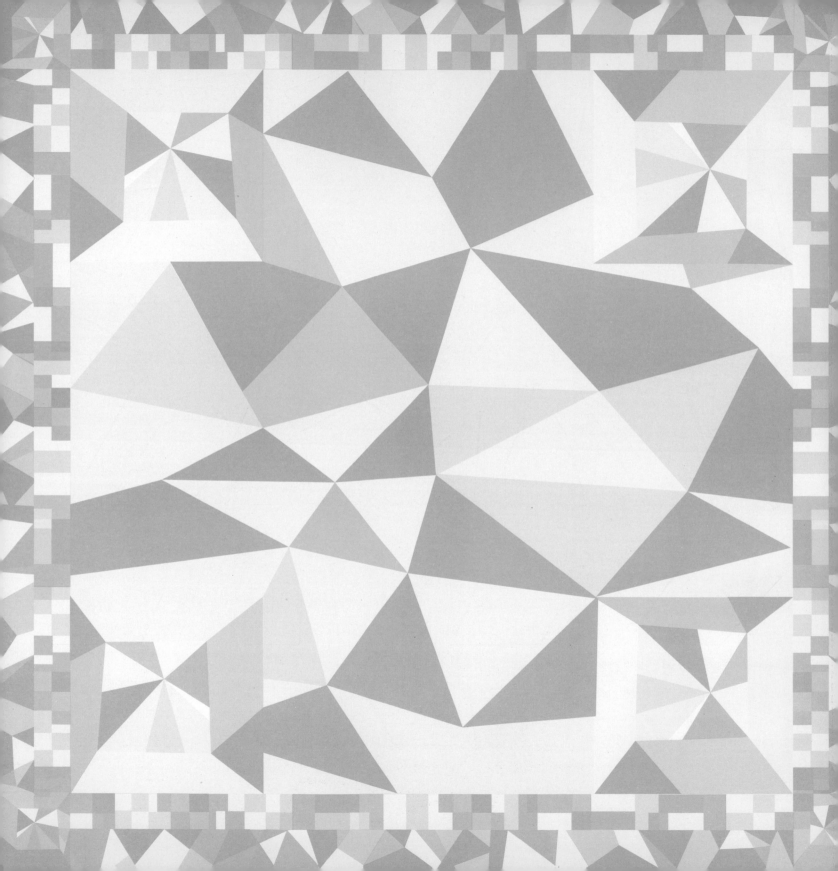

1   2   3   4   5   6   7

8   9   10   11   12   13   14   15   16

17   18   19   20   21   22   23   24

25   26   27   28   29   30   31   32

33   34   35   36   37   38

39   40   41   42   43   44   45

46   47   48   49   50   51   52

53   54   55   56   57   58   59   60   61   62   63

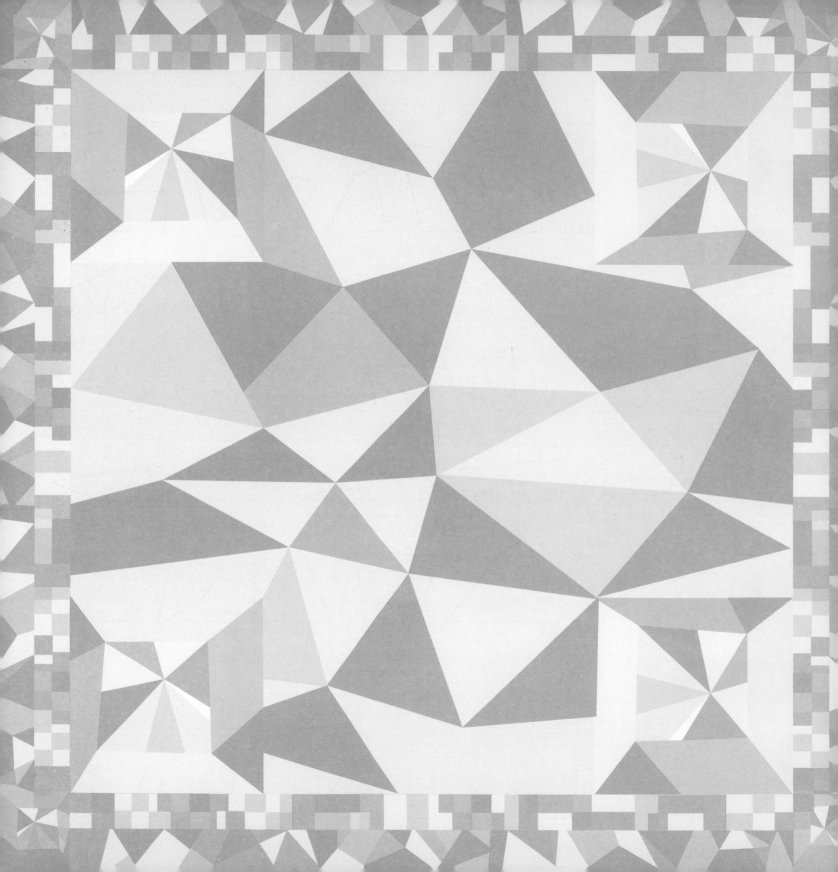

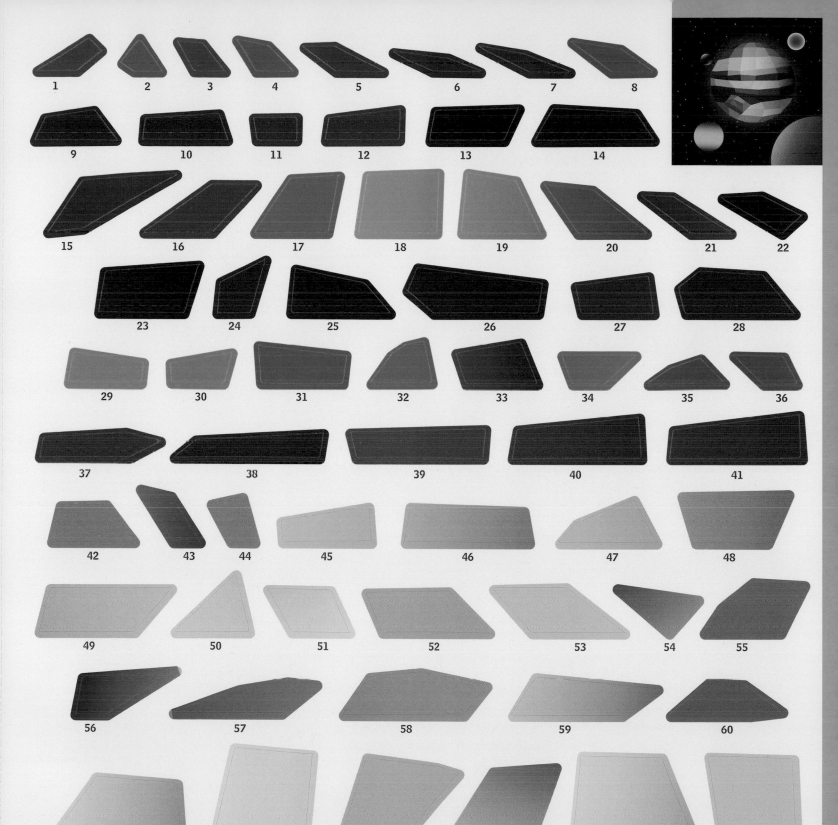

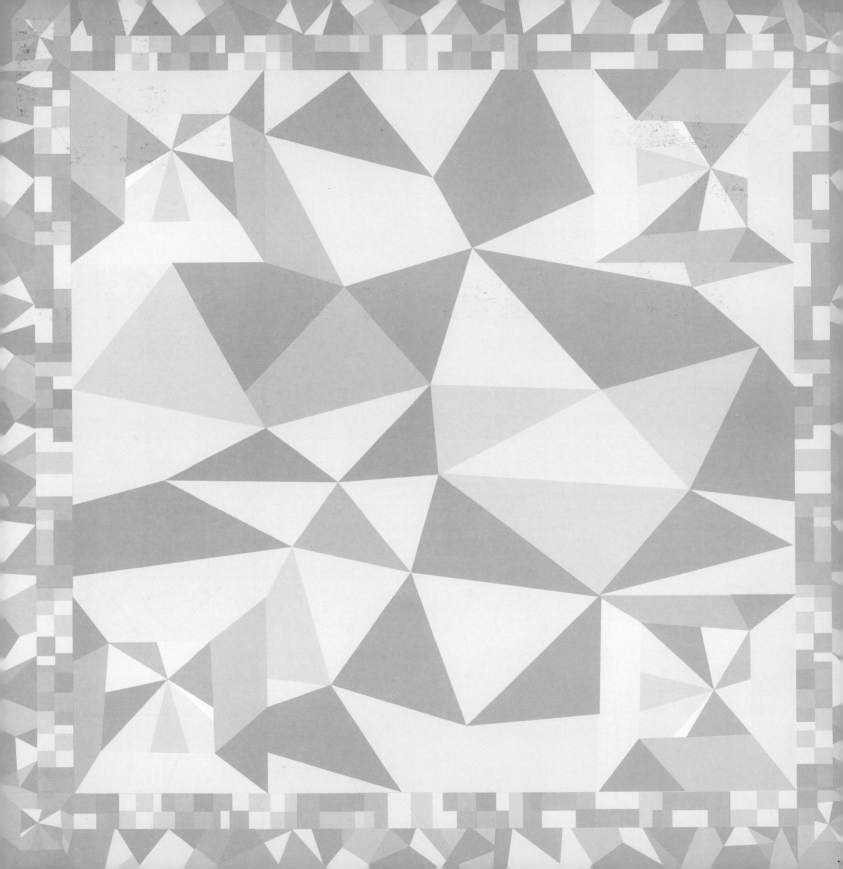

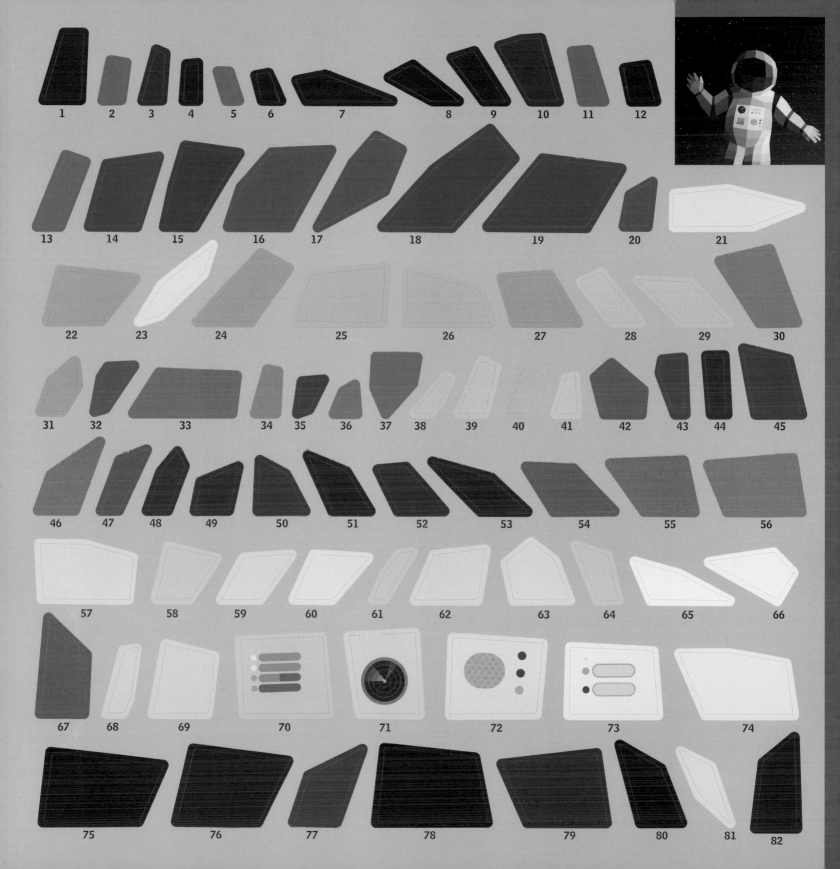

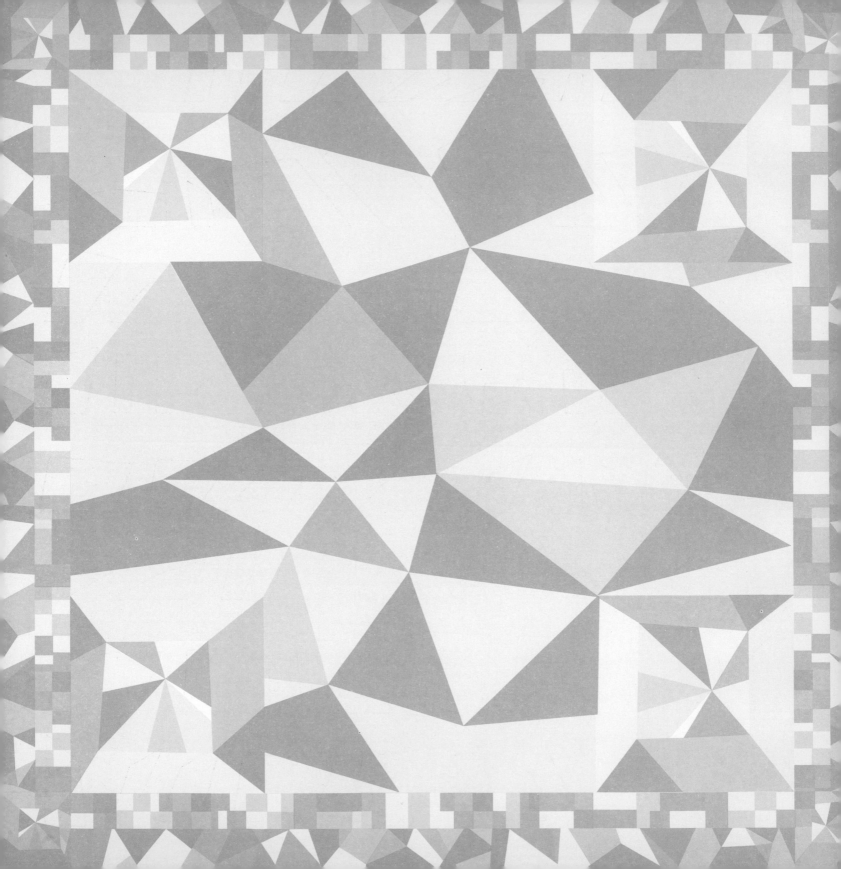

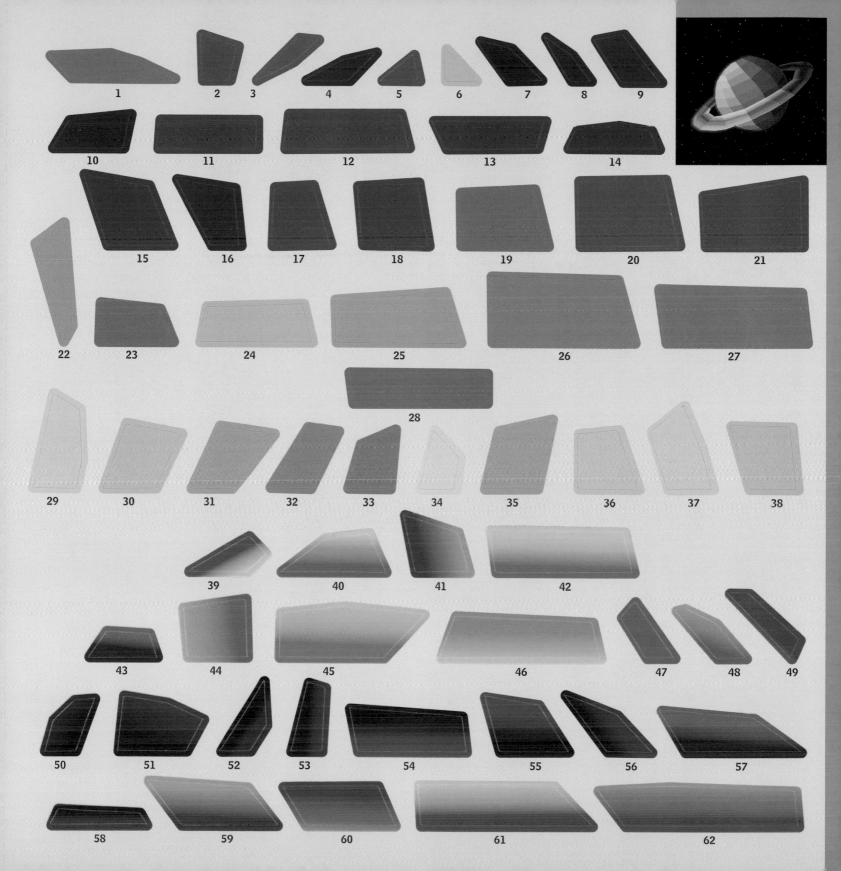

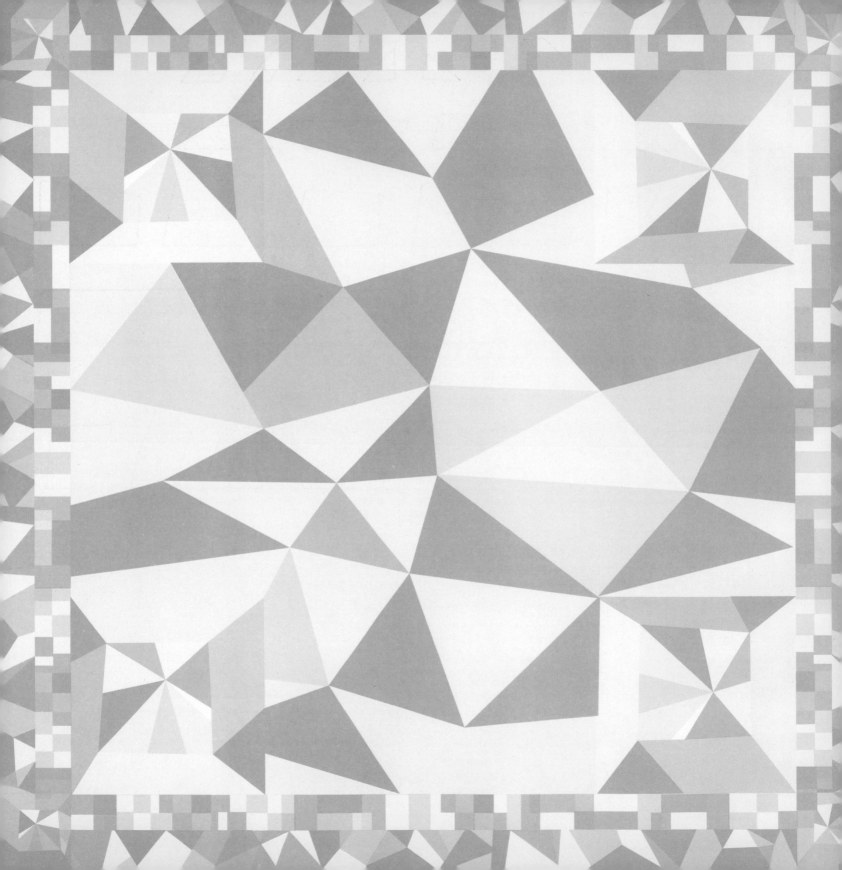

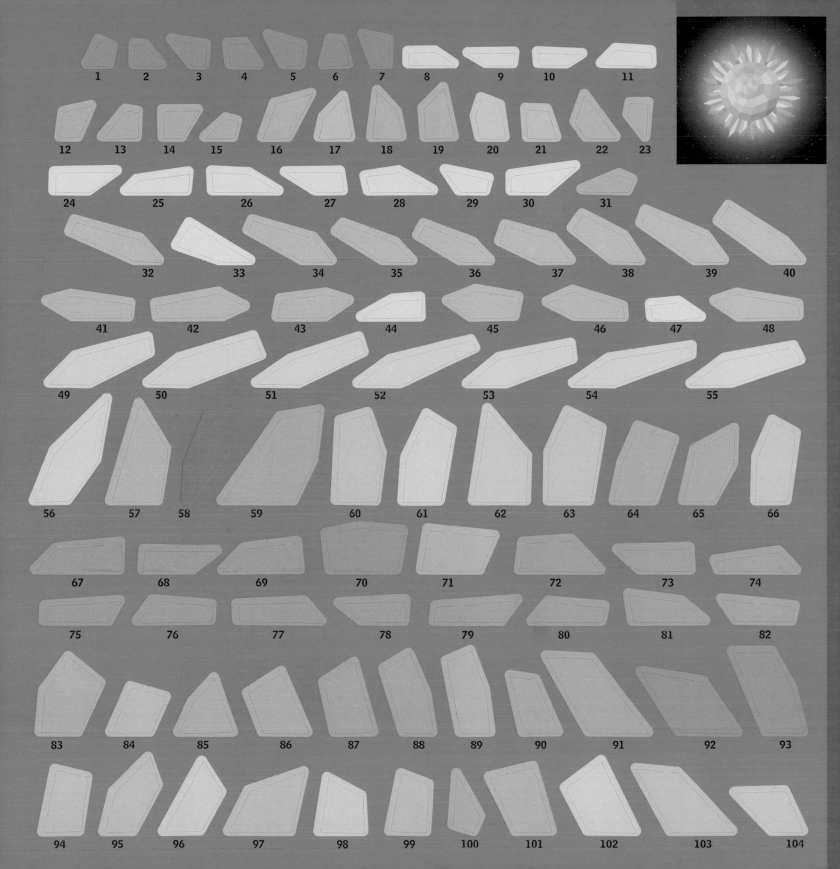

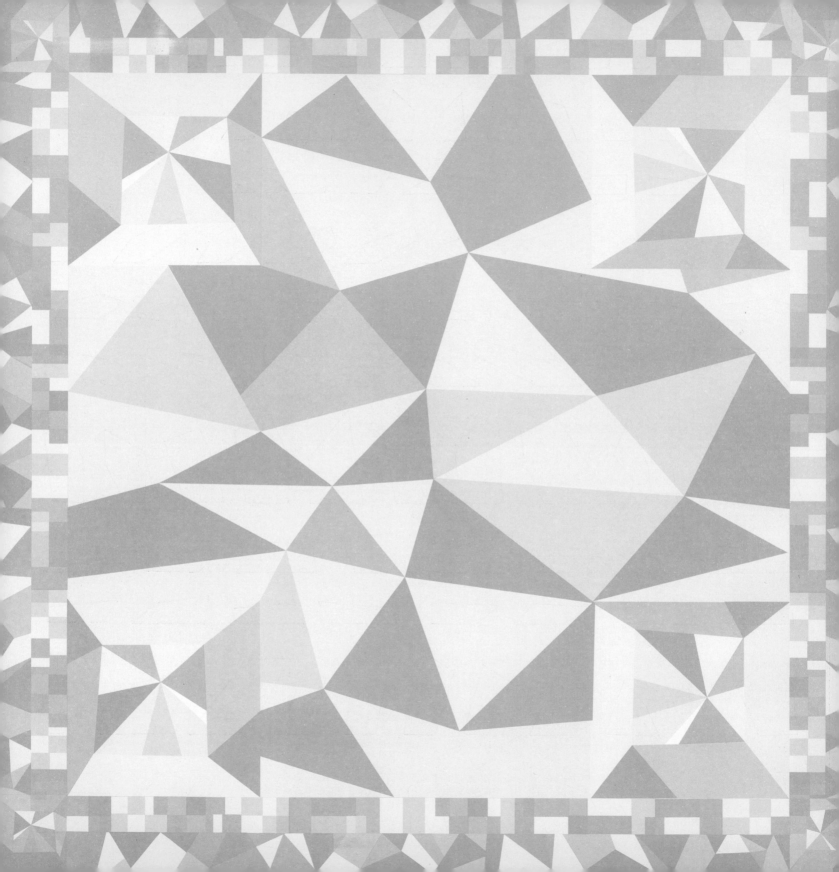

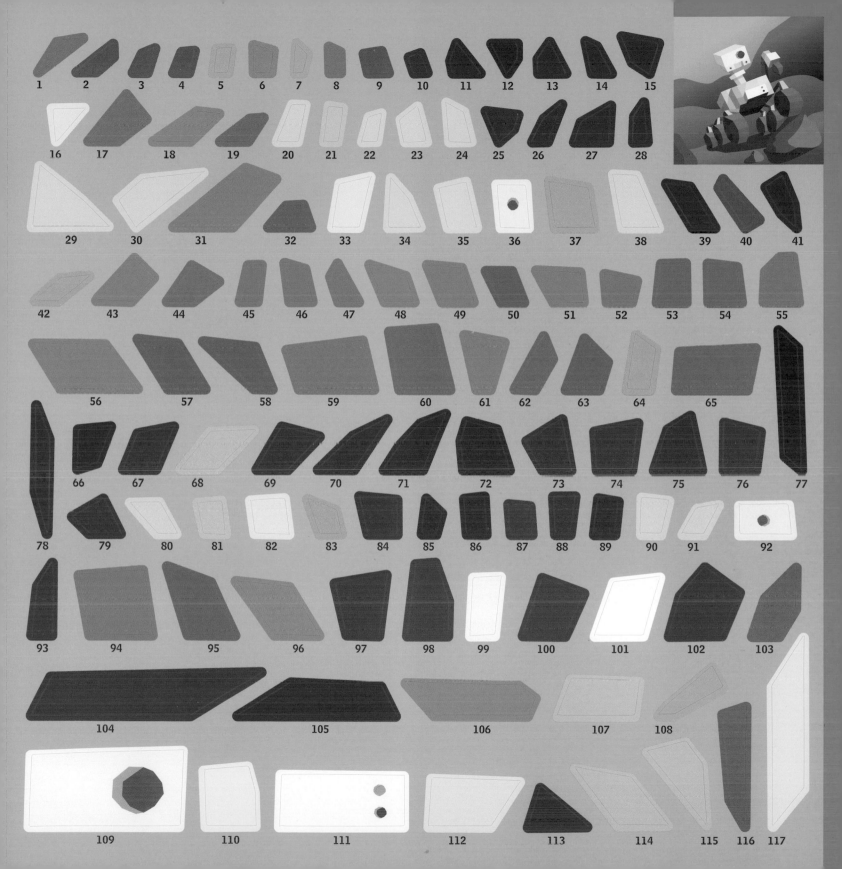

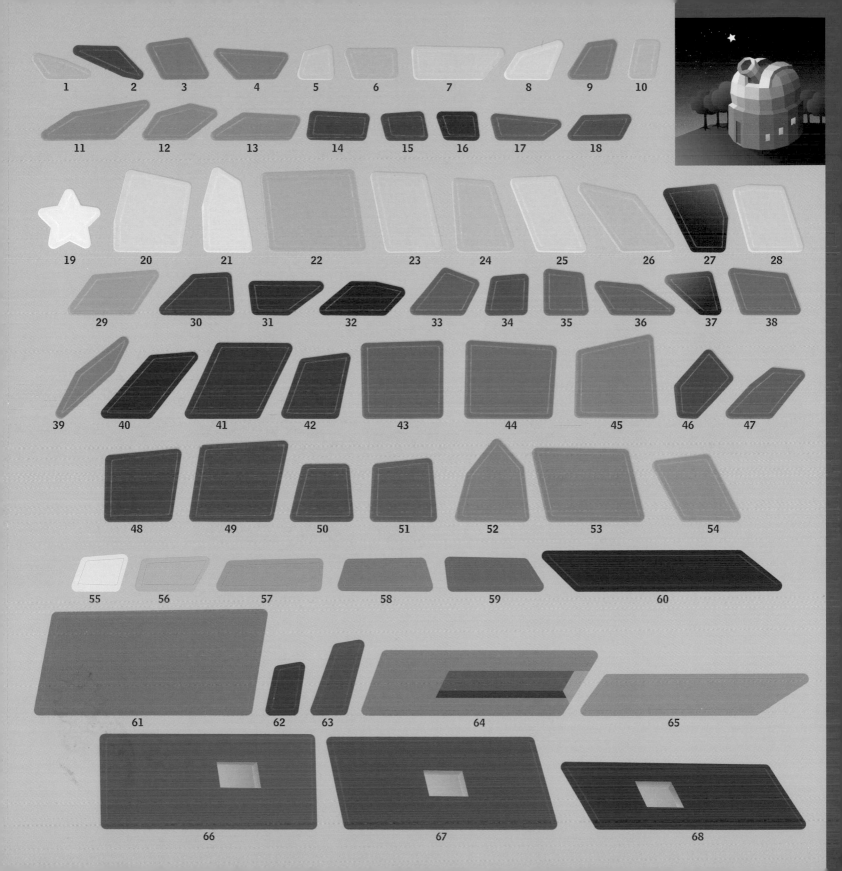

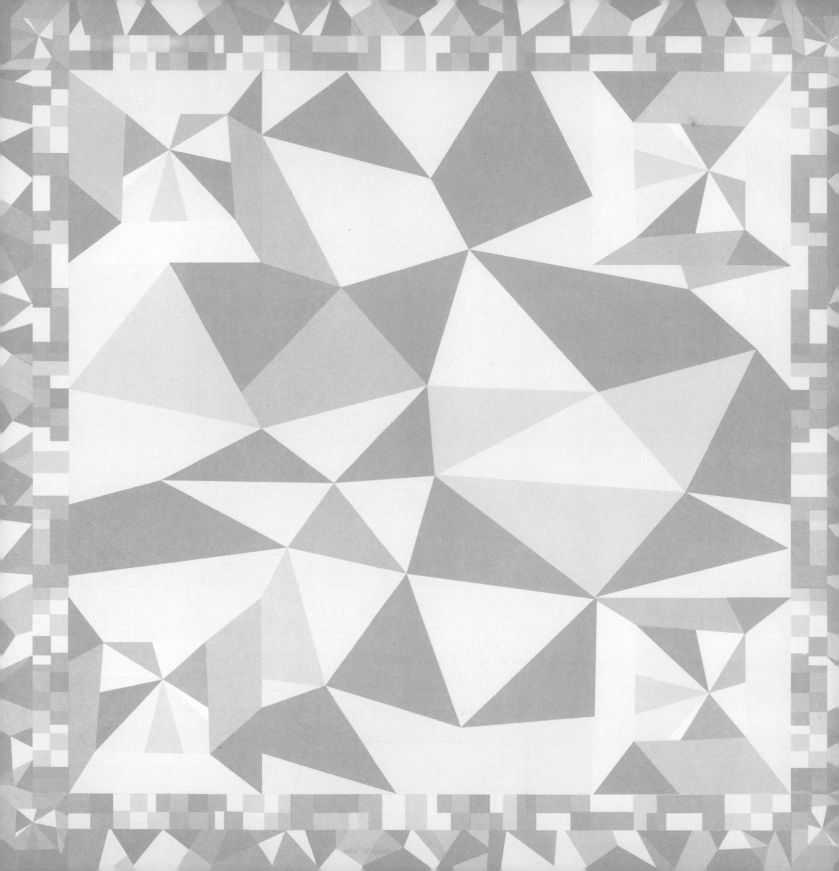

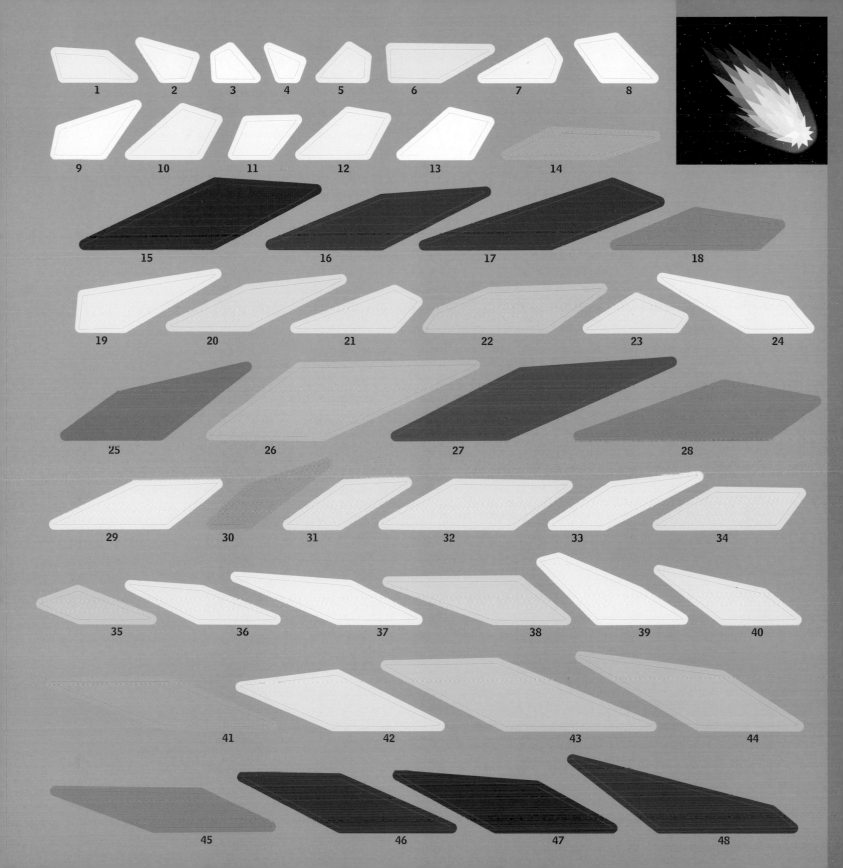

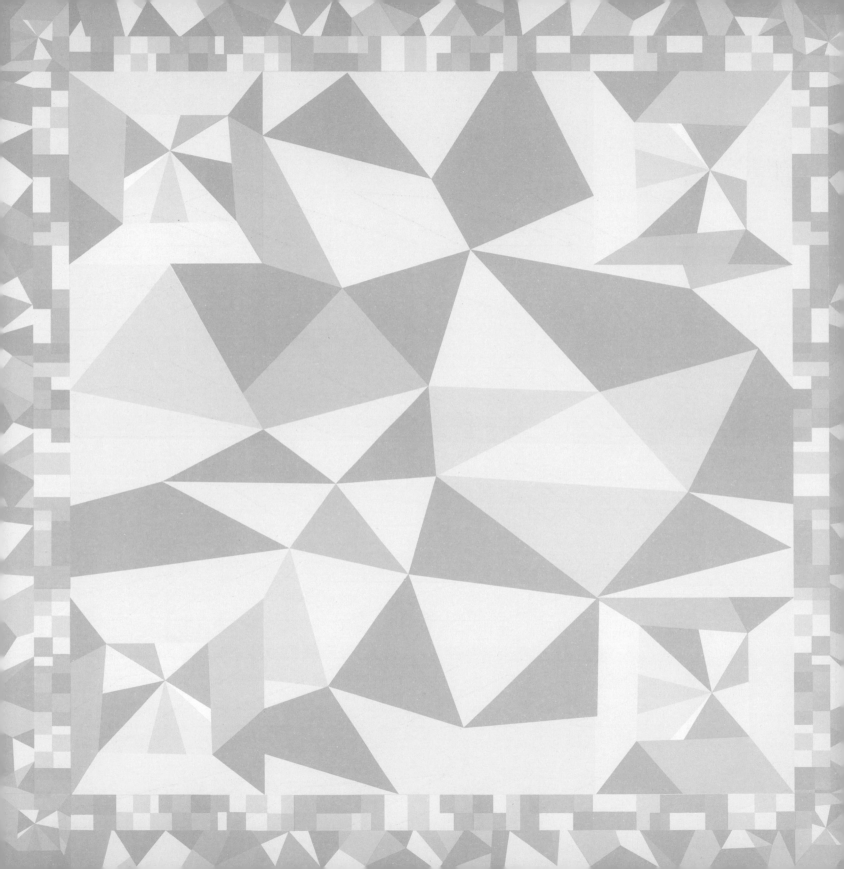